STEP-UP Books

are written especially for children who have outgrown
beginning readers. In this exciting series:

• the words are harder (but not too hard)
• there's more text (but it's still in big print)
• there are plenty of illustrations (but the books
aren't picture books)
• the subject matter has been carefully chosen to
appeal to young readers who want to find out about
the world around them.
They'll love these informative and lively books.

STAR WARS:
The Making of the Movie

Here is the story of how one of the most successful
motion pictures of all time was made:
• how the space battle scenes were filmed
• who was inside the robot suits
• what made the lightsabers glow
• what was the secret of Darth Vader
And much, much more!

STAR WARS™

The Making of the Movie

by LARRY WEINBERG

Step-Up Books   Random House
New York

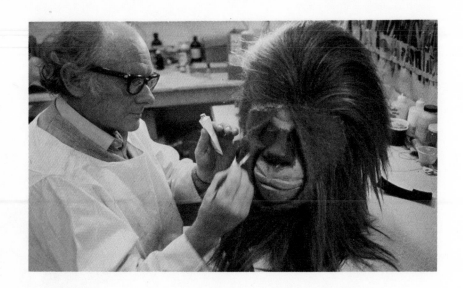

To Heather, Michael, and Lara

The author and editor wish to thank the people at Lucasfilm Ltd.—and most especially Diana Attias— for their help in producing this book.

Copyright © Lucasfilm Ltd. (LFL) 1980. All rights reserved under International and Pan-American Copyright Conventions. Published in the United States by Random House, Inc., New York, and simultaneously in Canada by Random House of Canada Limited, Toronto.
Library of Congress Cataloging in Publication Data:
Weinberg, Larry. Star wars. (Step-up books; no. 32) SUMMARY: Discusses how the movie "Star Wars" was made and how the special effects were created.
1. Star wars. (Motion picture)—Juvenile literature.   [1. Star wars. (Motion picture)]   I. Title.   PN1997.865943W4   791.43'72   80-13500
ISBN: 0-394-84493-9 (trade); 0-394-94493-3 (lib. bdg.)
Manufactured in the United States of America   1 2 3 4 5 6 7 8 9 0

Contents

Only Make-Believe?

The movie house is dark. Everyone is seated. Some people are talking. Others are eating candy and popcorn. Some are sitting quietly and waiting.

All of a sudden, the movie screen becomes outer space. "Star Wars" has begun! Soon a great planet begins to appear. Then a tiny spaceship races across the sky. Behind it is a giant battle cruiser. The cruiser is chasing the smaller ship—and firing at it. The tiny spacecraft is firing back. But it can't get away. One of the laser beams from the cruiser hits the smaller ship. BOOM! An explosion! The spaceship starts to fall apart.

Now everyone knows that this scene was make-believe. "Star Wars" was make-believe. But wait a minute. Was any of it real? The spaceships? The lasers? The explosions? And was the movie really made in outer space?

There are other questions too. Was Artoo-Detoo a real robot? Or was there somebody hiding inside? And those strange creatures from other planets! Where did **they** come from? How was "Star Wars" made?

Note: Do you remember the story of "Star Wars"? Yes? Then go on to the next chapter. No? Then turn to page 62.

What Makes a "Movie" Move

"Star Wars" was a very special movie. But it was the same as other movies in one way. It was made up of moving pictures. How do moving pictures work?

You probably have seen a camera that takes one picture at a time. You stand in front of it. Somebody says, "Don't move!" or "Smile!" Then it goes **click.** And later you see a picture of yourself, a photograph.

A movie camera also takes one picture at a time. But it takes a whole bunch of them in a row.

Pretend a movie camera is pointed at you. Say "One" aloud. But say it not too fast and not too slow.

Can you guess how many photographs the camera just took of you? Twenty-four in one second! Half of them were of your mouth opening to say "One." Half of them were of your mouth closing. Each picture showed your mouth opening a little bit more. Or closing a little bit more.

Imagine that you are holding those 24 pictures in your hand. They are one on top of the other. They are like a deck of cards. Flip those pictures of you saying "One." Do it very quickly. Guess what? Your mouth looks as if it is opening and closing. This is just like looking at a movie.

The movie you see in a theater is just a little different. There, the pictures are not held up in front of you. They are not in a stack like a deck of cards. They are all on a very long piece of film. The piece of film is behind you and high above you. It is in a machine called a projector. The projector has a light that shines through the film. It projects the pictures onto the screen.

The projector moves the film. And so the pictures on the screen seem to move too. What if the projector stopped? Then the

good guys would stop running. They would never get away from the bad guys.

Real Places

Was "Star Wars" made in space? Yes and no. The planet Earth is in space. Just like the other planets and stars are. The whole film was made here on Earth. It was made in different parts of our world.

Do you remember the farm that Luke lived on with his uncle and aunt? It was very hot and dusty there. Near the farm was a desert full of sand where Artoo-Detoo and See-Threepio landed. Close to the desert were rocky places where nothing grew. Someone special lived among those rocks— Obi-Wan Kenobi.

In the story, the farm and desert and rocky places were on a faraway planet. But these scenes were really made in Africa. The actors and the robots were brought there. They went to a country called Tunisia (too-NEE-shuh). It has a great sand desert called the Sahara. Tunisia has rocky places too. It looked just right to be Luke's planet.

Do you remember Luke's house? Luke didn't just walk straight into it. He didn't have stairs to climb up to it. He had to go **down** into it. His house was built inside a big hole in the ground!

Was that a made-up house? No. Luke's house is a real house. In fact, that house is a hotel in real life. People were coming there to stay long before "Star Wars" was ever made. The hotel is in a town full of other holes in the ground. They are all houses.

The town is called Matmata. And people have lived in those houses in the ground for hundreds of years.

Scene filmed inside a hotel in Matmata

Why were the houses built this way? Mostly to keep the people in the houses cool. Deserts get hot from the sun. There is no sun underground.

But not everything that was needed for "Star Wars" was already there. Some things had to be changed to fit the story. Builders had to put up a make-believe farm. The hotel had to be made to look like a home on a faraway planet. Luke's landspeeder had to be brought in.

There were problems in getting everything done. A big desert sandstorm got in the way. It blew the sand hard in everyone's face. They had to put on goggles to see.

Two months went by before everything was ready for filming. Then the actors began to act. And the cameras took pictures of them.

Make-Believe Places

After everyone was finished in Africa, they went to England. There, near the great city of London, is a film studio. It has buildings called stages. They are so big that all kinds of make-believe places can be built inside them. These places are called sets.

Have you ever been to a play in your school? If you have, you may have seen a set. It is a make-believe place that is built on the stage. And it is just for the actors to act the story in. It can look like a forest. Or the inside of a castle. Or anything else. It is built just for the play. When it is not needed anymore, it is taken down.

Some sets were built just for "Star Wars" too. Whenever you saw anyone **inside** a spaceship or the Death Star, you were looking at a set.

There were a lot of sets for the Death Star. Do you remember the room where the walls were closing in? Luke, Leia, Han, and Chewie were trapped in it. There was a lot of water and garbage in the room too. A monster was swimming under the water. It reached up and curled around Luke's leg.

A "Star Wars" set

Then it pulled him under into all that wet, smelly, awful slime. Eeeyuk!

Well, the room wasn't a real place. It was a set. So were the halls where Han Solo blasted the bad guys. And where Darth Vader fought Obi-Wan Kenobi. The place where Han's ship was trapped was a set too.

There were many other sets in "Star Wars." Thirty-six of them all together.

A set being built

Most of "Star Wars" was made in them.

Not only were there make-believe **places** in the movie. There were also a lot of make-believe **things.** Most of these were made inside a big building in the state of California. In the movie, you saw them flashing through outer space. What were they?

Turn the page and find out.

Spaceships

The things that you saw flash through space were real spaceships. Right? Wrong! All the spaceships in "Star Wars" were models. Most of them were very small. The space fighters that fought each other over the Death Star were the size of toys. They were no more than one and a half feet long. The battle cruiser that chased Leia's ship at the beginning of "Star Wars" was a little bigger. It was about three feet long.

But they were not little models of real spaceships. They were all invented just for "Star Wars." First, drawings were made of what they ought to look like. Then the ships had to be built very carefully. Each model was put together from many little parts. Some of these parts were made just for the movie. But other parts came from model kits. They were the kind of kits you can buy in a hobby store.

Everything was put together in the special workshop for "Star Wars" in California. Seventy-five different kinds of models were used in the movie. There were also some extra models.

The extra models had a special use. Sometimes a spaceship had to be exploded. So one of the copies was blown up. Each copy had an opening on one side. A tiny bomb was placed in the opening. Later, the bomb would go off. A camera would take pictures of the explosion. In the movie you thought a spaceship was hit by lasers. But really, a model was blown up from inside.

All the models were made to look like real spaceships. They seemed to zoom all over the galaxy (GAL-uck-see). But the truth is that not one of the models could fly! They had to be held up in front of the camera on metal sticks. Of course, the sticks did not show in the movie.

The filming of an explosion

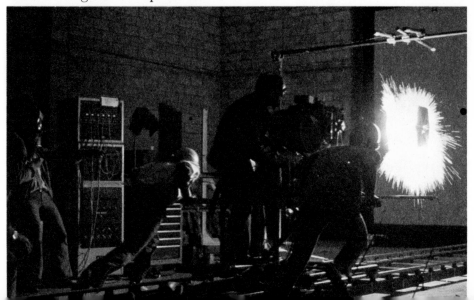

A model held up by a metal stick

The models could be made to turn a little. But that was all they could do. The camera had you fooled.

The Flying Camera

"Stars Wars" had a very special camera. It was used to film the little models. It made them look much bigger than they were. And it also made them look as if they were flying.

As the camera took pictures, it kept moving. Movie people say it was "traveling." Sometimes it went away from a model, backward. Sometimes it went diving under one. On the screen it looked as if the model were flying and climbing and diving. How could that be?

Have you ever been on a merry-go-round? Most of the time there are parents standing around it. They are watching the children go round and round. The children are also watching their parents. To the moving children, the parents seem to be moving too. As the children move one way, the parents seem to move the other way. The faster the merry-go-round moves, the faster the parents go by. Even though the parents are really standing still.

The camera in "Star Wars" was like a child on a merry-go-round. When it went one way, the models looked as if they were going the other way. They weren't. The model spaceships stayed in the same place, just as the parents did.

The camera was held up on the end of a long metal arm. The arm moved the camera as your arm and hand would move a toy

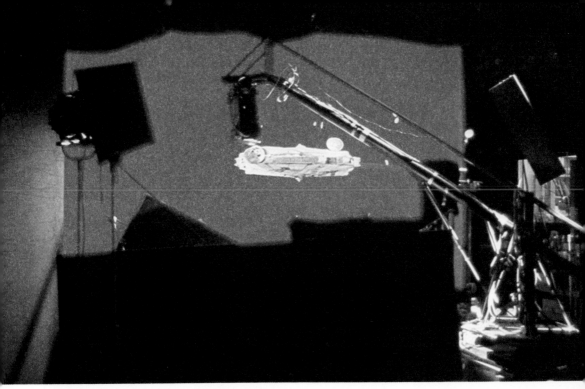

The camera on the end of a long arm

airplane. But the camera had something you don't have. It had a computer to tell it what to do.

The camera was very special, all right. But there is one thing it could not do. It could not take pictures of two spacecraft flying at the same time.

Then what about all those great space battles? How were they made?

Space Fights

A Rebel fighter heads straight for the Death Star. One of Darth Vader's TIE fighters comes flying to stop it. Both sides blast lasers at each other. They miss! The Rebel craft dives to get away. The enemy dives after it. The Rebel ship comes up fast behind the enemy ship—and blows it up!

There were many fights like that in "Star Wars." Only none of them ever really happened. How could they? The models could not fly. And the camera could only shoot pictures of one of them at a time. Then how were the fight scenes done?

First the camera took moving pictures of just the Rebel space fighter. There was nothing else in the picture. The camera made the Rebel space fighter model look as

if it were flying. Then the camera took
moving pictures of the enemy TIE fighter. It
was all by itself. The camera also made that
model look like it was flying.

Then the camera took pictures of the
Death Star model alone.

Then it took pictures of some stars.

All the pieces of the film were put into a machine. They were put one on top of the other. This machine takes pictures too. Only it takes pictures of other pictures. When it was finished, there was a brand-new piece of film. Guess what? All four scenes were now in the same picture.

So the fighters and the laser blasts and the Death Star never met. Only their photographs met in the machine that mixed them all together. They each fitted into an empty part of the new picture.

The Death Star

The round ship that Darth Vader and his men traveled on was called the Death Star. It could destroy anything that got in its way.

It looked so big that Luke first thought it was a moon! How big was it really? As big as a real moon? Nope. Was it as big as Artoo-Detoo? Well, just a little bit bigger. The Death Star that Luke and his friends first saw was only four feet across. That's not much larger than a beach ball!

That was the model of the whole Death Star. There were also some models of parts of it. They were used mostly to film the final space battle.

The picture below shows a tiny explosion on a Death Star model. In the movie, this explosion looked much bigger. You thought a blast from a space fighter caused it. But there are no space fighters here. The fighters had to be mixed into the picture later. The explosion was set off by someone pressing a button. Then a little bomb went off inside the model. The bomb was filled with kerosene and black powder.

And where was this part of the great battle really filmed? Look closely. Do you see a truck parked right nearby? This explosion on the Death Star took place in a parking lot! The lot was just outside the building where the models were kept. The camera was moved outdoors. The light outside was best for taking these pictures.

Of course, you never saw the parking lot in "Star Wars." The special camera kept **that** out of the picture. If it had not, you might have seen a truck in the middle of a space battle!

In the movie, the explosion in this photo did not make the whole Death Star blow up. It blew up only a small piece. Do you remember when Luke **did** blow up the whole Death Star? You saw that happen, right? Or did you?

Guess what? Your eyes were fooled again. The Death Star model never exploded at all. The cameraman filmed another explosion. The pictures of that explosion were mixed with a picture of the Death Star model. On the screen, it looked like bits of the Death Star flew through the sky. But the bits were not from the Death Star at all. They were just sawdust.

So what became of the real Death Star? Be careful, kids. It still exists.

How Would You Like to Be in "Star Wars"?

Where are you right now? Are you in a room? How would you like to be standing next to Obi-Wan Kenobi in the middle of "Star Wars"? Would you mind that he is way, way up inside the Death Star? And in danger of falling to his doom?

Don't be afraid. Obi-Wan Kenobi isn't there either. He is standing only three feet above the floor of another room!

The camera took moving pictures of him pretending to be high up. He was supposed to be turning off the tractor beam. Then other pictures were taken of a painting. It was made on a piece of glass by an artist. The painting showed the high wall. It left a space for Kenobi and the control tower.

Then the two sets of pictures were taken to the print shop. There they were put together into one picture. It was the picture you saw on page 37.

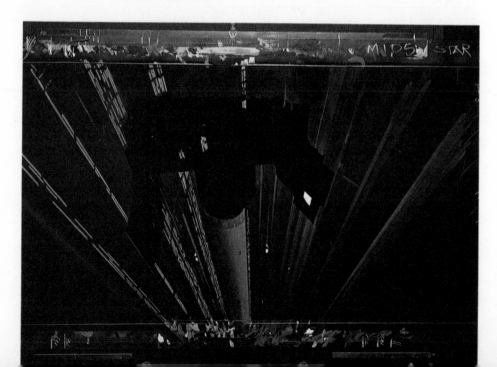

The same thing could be done with you too. A photo could be taken of you where you are right now. Then your picture could be put together with Obi-Wan Kenobi's picture. It would look as if you were up there with him. Your own room would be gone.

And you too would be in danger of falling down, down, down.

The Lightsabers

Once upon a time, a Jedi Knight named Darth Vader turned to evil. He killed many good Jedis. A long time later, he met a Jedi who had escaped Vader's evil. It was Obi-Wan Kenobi. And they fought with swords that shined and hummed like laser beams.

Were these swords really laser swords? No, they were not.

Have you ever held a mirror in your hand? You may have bounced sunlight off it. Maybe you flashed signals with it. Or made the sun shine on a wall.

By now you may have guessed. The sword blades worked like mirrors. They were made of tiny glass beads glued to a rod. The beads were much shinier than a regular mirror.

To make the blades shine, the swords had
to spin. Tiny motors in the sword handles
turned the blades. Then the glass beads
would catch the light. The light came from
a lamp. It was placed just above the camera
that took pictures of the fight. Then the
swords glowed as brightly as lasers.

The Secret of Darth Vader

Darth Vader had a secret. What was it?
Here is a hint. What you saw you didn't
hear. What you heard you didn't see.
Give up?

Two people played Darth Vader! One
person was inside the mask. The other
person said all his words. The one you saw
was never **heard** in "Star Wars." The one
you heard was never **seen** in "Star Wars."

The actor you heard was an American named James Earl Jones. The actor you saw was an Englishman named David Prowse. He used to be the best weight-lifter in England. That may have helped him in the movie. The suit he wore was pretty heavy. It was made of lots of leather and canvas. Part of it was even made of metal. The suit made Mr. Prowse tired.

At first he had trouble with the mask. It was very loose. When he tried to turn his head, the mask would not move. That problem was fixed. Some foam rubber was put inside the mask. But something that fixes one problem often starts another. All

David Prowse
(in red) practices
dueling with
Alec Guinness.

that rubber made him sweat and sweat
when he tried to fight Alec Guinness. Alec
Guinness is the man who played Obi-Wan
Kenobi.

Do you remember when Darth Vader
made fun of Obi-Wan Kenobi? "Your
powers are weak, old man," he said.

That may be. But guess who had to keep
stopping to rest in the middle of the fight?
Darth Vader! (You didn't see **that** in the
movie.) Maybe Vader was saving his
strength for the next "Star Wars" movie.

Do you want to see him with his mask
off? He's right here at the top of the page.

Artoo-Detoo (R2-D2)

Was Artoo-Detoo a real robot?
Yes, he was. And no, he wasn't.
Sometimes you saw a real robot. In fact,
there were a few real robots who played
Artoo. They had lots of wires inside them.
They could be made to do different things.
One robot was used to go from place to

place. It had wheels underneath. You could not see them. That was the robot that the Jawas shot. Another robot had a special arm. It was used to plug into the controls on the Death Star. There was even one Artoo that was only one inch high!

But most of the time, Artoo was hollow. And there was a little man inside. Here he is!

His name is Kenny Baker. He is only 38 inches high. That is about the size of a child in the third grade. But he is a grown man. He is not only an actor. He has also been a musician and a circus clown.

Kenny didn't make any of Artoo's noises. And he couldn't move around in Artoo very well either. But he could make parts of the robot's head spin. And he could rock from side to side on Artoo's legs.

When Kenny didn't need to rock, he could sit down. He could do this even though Artoo was standing. Kenny had a little seat inside.

See-Threepio (C-3PO)

Everybody knows that See-Threepio wasn't a real robot. They know that he was a man inside a robot suit. What they don't know is what he really looks like. Here he is!

His real name is Anthony Daniels. "Not that anybody cares!" says Anthony. He is an actor from England.

His robot suit was very heavy. It weighed 50 pounds. And it was very hot inside. "It was just terrible when we were in the desert," said Anthony. "I thought I would bake like a cake!"

The suit took a long time to get into and out of. Anthony had to stay in it for hours and hours. Sometimes people forgot that he wasn't a robot. And sometimes they remembered to give him some water through a straw. "At last!"

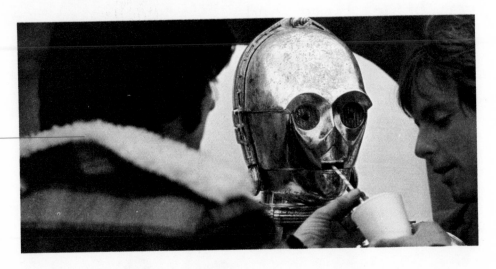

The suit had little openings that Anthony could see out of. But he could not see very well. He had trouble turning his head. And he had to see around the little light bulbs that were stuck in front of his eyes.

The suit was impossible to sit down in!
They had to give Anthony a board to lean
on. Everyone else had a chair! Even Kenny
Baker could sit down **inside** Artoo. All this
made Anthony cranky sometimes. Then he
could **really** tell Artoo how silly he was!

And, oh dear, poor Threepio. He
sometimes forgot that the robot suit was
taller than he was. That was all right
when he was outside in the desert. But that
was not so fine going into a house. It was a
good way to bump his head on the doorway!

The Creature Bar

Do you remember the bar where they refused to serve robots? But they didn't mind serving monsters! Where did all those monsters come from? Other planets?

No. Most of them were people wearing monster suits. The bar was like one big Halloween party.

A few of the masks they wore had been made years before. They had been made for other movies. But nobody had used them for a long time. They were just sitting on a shelf getting dusty. One of these was a werewolf mask. Have you ever watched a scary movie on TV? Perhaps you saw one of the werewolf's relatives.

Other masks were made just for "Star Wars." An artist drew a picture of what they ought to look like. Then a few people helped to make them. Most of the masks were made of rubber and plastic.

Everyone had to hurry to get the masks finished. And once in a while a mistake was made. Remember the musicians with the big heads? The ones who looked alike?

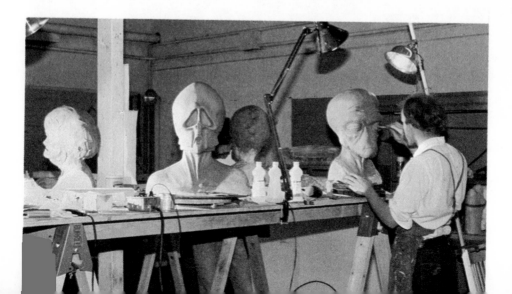

Well, they all had the same problem. No noses. Each mask did have a tiny hole for a mouth. But that wasn't enough to breathe through. Some of the musicians played flutes or oboes. When they did, the little hole got covered. That made it even harder to breathe. Finally, someone cut more holes to let air in. But by then, some of the players had to be given oxygen (OCK-sih-jun).

By the way, they didn't really play any music. They only acted as if they did. The music was added to the film later.

Still More Monsters

There were other monsters in "Star Wars." Very little ones. They were the chess pieces in the game that Artoo played with Chewie. Artoo was winning. And Han Solo said, "Let him have it. It's not wise to upset a Wookiee." Remember?

These little monsters were really models. They had metal frames inside. But their skin was made of rubber. Eight of them were used in the game. It took two people to make them move.

In the movie, the game was played in Han's spaceship. But it didn't really happen that way. First the camera took moving pictures of Artoo and Chewie playing without models. Then the model game was filmed all by itself. Later the two films were put together into one. And you could see through the chess pieces! There is a very long word for this trick. It is called superimposing (soo-per-im-POZE-ing).

In the movie, the chess game lasted only a few minutes. But its filming took many hours. The monsters could be moved only when the camera was not taking pictures. So the camera had to stop and start, stop and start. Each time the camera stopped, the models were moved. But each move was very tiny. Part of a hand here. Part of a leg there. Then the camera would take another picture. It would stop again. Then someone would move the hand and the leg just a little bit more. Then the camera would shoot again. This went on and on. At last all the moves of all the monsters were filmed.

When you went to the movie, you didn't see people moving the monster models. And you didn't see the camera keep stopping to let them do it. It looked as if the little monsters were moving all by themselves.

Languages

We don't know who or what lives on other planets. But there is one thing we can be sure of. They don't speak English. English is an Earth language. And even most people on Earth don't speak it.

Why did people in "Star Wars" speak English? So that we could understand the movie, of course. But there were a lot of other languages heard in "Star Wars" too. Artoo spoke in beeps and squeaks. The Wookiee spoke in roars and honks. The little Jawas said, "Jabber, jabber, jabber." Where did these strange sounds come from?

Some of Artoo's sounds were made on an electronic (ih-leck-TRON-ick) machine. Some of his other sounds were made by a person. His whistling sound came from a person blowing into a water pipe. And a scraping sound came from rubbing ice against metal. These sounds were all mixed together and put on a recording machine. Later, they were played when it was Artoo's turn to speak.

What kinds of sounds did Chewie make?

Artoo-Detoo's sounds were
electronic.

The actor who played Chewbacca
never made a Wookiee sound.

Here is a hint. The actor who played
Chewie never made a Wookiee sound. No
human being ever did.

Chewie sounded mostly like a bear. That's
because what you heard **was** a bear! But you
heard other animal sounds too. There were
sea lions and walruses! Camels and cougars!
The "Star Wars" sound person made many
trips to the zoo to find these animals.

He recorded their noises on a tape recorder. Later, they were played aloud whenever Chewie had something to say.

The Jawas were those little fellows who caught Artoo and Threepio. They did not speak a real Earth language. Their words were from a lot of different languages all mixed together.

The "Star Wars" That Might Have Been

Is Chewie, the Wookiee, one of the good guys or the bad guys? Good guy? Well, he wasn't always.

You see, "Star Wars" was made up by a man named George Lucas. Mr. Lucas wrote other "Star Wars" stories before he picked the one you saw in the movie. In the first story, there was no Darth Vader. And there was no Death Star either. Who were the evil ones? A whole planet full of Wookiees!

The Wookiees looked a lot different from the Chewie we know. They looked meaner and a lot more like cats. Suppose that movie of "Star Wars" had been made? Here is what Chewie might have looked like.

In that story, the Wookiees rode around on giant birds. The big battle would have been fought on the Wookiee planet. And Luke would have had to beat 300 scary Wookiees to win that fight!

But then, Luke might not have been Luke. In the second story Luke was changed into a girl.

Han Solo looked old enough to be "Princess Luke's" father.

She was a princess who was trying to rescue her brother. She hired Han Solo to help her. Han looked different, though. He was old enough to be her father in that story.

Then Mr. Lucas changed the story again. He decided to make the picture about Artoo and Threepio. But later, he thought that would not be right either. The film ought to be about human beings. Even if they are from another part of the galaxy. But he still liked Artoo and Threepio very much. So he kept them in the story.

So now Luke is the boy. Leia is the girl. Han is young enough to be her boyfriend. That makes Luke mad! Chewie is cuddly. Darth Vader is the meanie. The Death Star is the worst weapon the galaxy has ever seen.

And lots of people love the movie.

Till the Empire Strikes Back!

"Star Wars" had a lot of fighting in it. It had a lot of guns and battles. It had lasers and explosions too. People got shot and fell down. But the truth is that nobody was ever really hurt. Not the actors or anybody who worked on the film.

62

The reason "Star Wars" was so much fun was that people had fun making it. They cared about "Star Wars" and about each other.

See you at the next "Star Wars" movie!!

The Story of "Star Wars"

Once upon a spaceship long ago and far away, there was a princess. Her name was Leia. An evil man named Darth Vader was chasing her in his battle cruiser. Princess Leia had the secret plans of the Death Star. And Vader wanted them back.

Pictures on page 63: **1.** Obi-Wan Kenobi, **2.** Death Star, **3.** Artoo-Detoo, **4.** Darth Vader, **5.** See-Threepio, **6.** Princess Leia.

1

2

3

4

5

6

The Death Star was a big space station that could destroy anything. It had been made by the evil people who ruled the Empire. Leia belonged to the Rebels. They were trying to stop the Empire. She wanted to give the Rebel leaders the plans to the Death Star. Those plans could help them blow it up before it could hurt anyone.

Vader captured Princess Leia. But he didn't get the plans from her. She gave them to a robot named Artoo-Detoo (R2-D2). She also gave Artoo a message for a Jedi Knight named Obi-Wan Kenobi. Artoo escaped with another robot. His name was See-Threepio (C-3PO).

The two robots landed on a planet. They were captured by a group of little creatures called Jawas. The Jawas sold the robots to a farmer. On the farm lived a young man named Luke Skywalker.

Artoo ran away from the farm. He went looking for Obi-Wan Kenobi. Then Luke and See-Threepio had to go looking for Artoo. But as soon as they found Artoo, they were attacked by some Sandpeople. An old man saved them. He was Obi-Wan Kenobi.

Artoo gave Kenobi the message from Princess Leia. She asked him to take the plans to the Rebels. Kenobi said he would. And he wanted Luke to help him.

Kenobi told Luke about the Force. "It is an energy field. It is all around us," Kenobi said. "Jedis know how to make it work. It gives us power. You can learn to make it work for you too. Your father did. He was a Jedi Knight."

The escape in Han Solo's ship

The two men and the robots went off to find a spaceship. They met a pilot named Han Solo. He was with his friend Chewbacca, a Wookiee. Han and Chewie helped them escape from Darth Vader's soldiers. Then they took off in Han's spaceship.

Soon battle cruisers were chasing them. But Solo was too fast for them. And they got away from the cruisers too. Finally, they felt safe.

But not for long. Right in front of them was the Death Star! They tried to escape from it. But the Death Star had a special kind of tractor beam. This beam pulled things inside the Death Star. And that is just what happened to Han Solo's ship. It got trapped! And in it were Han, Luke, Chewie, and the robots.

But Han had a secret hiding place on his ship. He and the others hid. So the Empire soldiers could not find them.

Later, the men and robots sneaked out of Han's ship. Obi-Wan Kenobi went to turn off the tractor beam. Luke and Han dressed up as Empire soldiers. With Chewie, they went to rescue Princess Leia. She was on the Death Star too. They found her. But soldiers chased them. Luke, Han, and Chewie tried to get back to Han Solo's spaceship. But other soldiers were standing in front of it.

Just then, Darth Vader found Obi-Wan Kenobi. The two men fought. The soldiers guarding Han's spaceship went to watch. That left Luke and the others free to get on the ship. Kenobi saw that his friends could get away. So he stopped fighting. Darth Vader hit him with his lightsaber. But when Vader looked for Obi-Wan Kenobi's body, he could not find it!

The others left safely. They flew to the Rebel base with the plans. The Death Star followed them there. The Rebel general studied the plans. He found out how the Death Star could be blown up. Rebel craft took off to attack the Death Star. Darth Vader sent out TIE fighters to fire back. The battle was on. Many Rebel ships were shot down. But Luke's was not.

In one of the Empire's TIE fighters was Darth Vader himself. He came up right

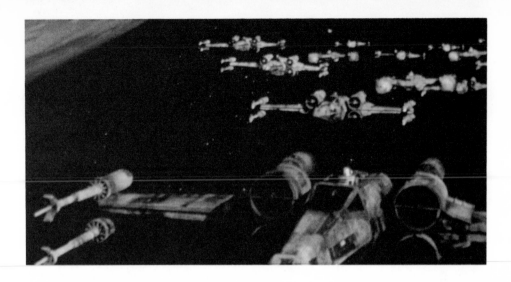

behind Luke. Vader was just about to shoot Luke's craft to bits. Suddenly, Han Solo's spaceship was there behind Vader. Han sent Vader's ship into a spin. Luke was free now to shoot at the Death Star. The Force was with him. He blew the Death Star into a million pieces!

Later, Luke and Han were given medals by the princess and the Rebel general. Artoo, Threepio, and Chewie watched. And everyone lived happily ever after. Until the evil Empire struck back!

Now turn back to page 10.

ABOUT THE AUTHOR

Larry Weinberg is a lawyer and a playwright as well as a writer of books for children. He is also writing a young adult novel with his sixteen-year-old daughter and an adult novel all by himself. He would like to write songs too. But, he complains, he can't carry a tune.

Mr. Weinberg loves the movie "Star Wars" and has seen it at least five times. He also loves kids. For those two reasons, he had a grand time writing this book.

Mr. Weinberg lives in the quiet town of Woodstock, New York.

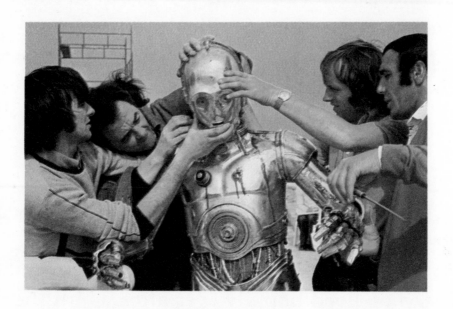